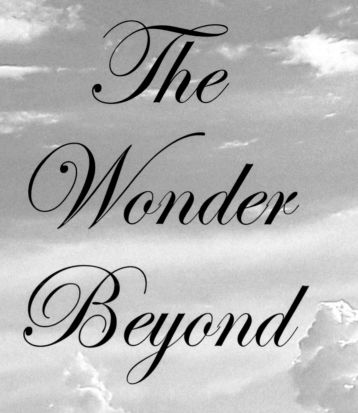

The Wonder Beyond

Lorner J. Jones

AuthorHouse™
1663 Liberty Drive
Bloomington, IN 47403
www.authorhouse.com
Phone: 833-262-8899

Scripture taken from the King James Version of the Bible.

This book is printed on acid-free paper.

ISBN: 978-1-6655-4723-9 (sc)
ISBN: 978-1-6655-4724-6 (e)

Library of Congress Control Number: 2021925108

Print information available on the last page.

Published by AuthorHouse 01/25/2022

authorHOUSE®

May God truly bless you

Lorner J. Jones

The Wonder Beyond

There is a beauty behind the clouds to see
It was promise to you, and also to me
When Jesus left he said he would come back
He stated be ye ready for we don't have to pack
There is place which you will never grow old
It's beautiful there with streets of pure gold
Rubies and diamond as far as you can see
Twelve gates to the cities is where we want to be
Precious stones are garnished about all the walls
The foundation fill with jasper, sapphire, and more as it stands tall
Every gate is of one pearl with transparent glass
This will be your new home forever it will last
So just know when we no longer need the sun nor the moon
The son of man is coming he will be here soon
They will be coming from the north, south, east, and west
To a city built foursquare I will do my best
Also remember that every word of God is always true
That the wonder beyond the clouds is waiting for you

*Ecclesiastes 1: 5 The sun also ariseth, and the sun goeth
down, and hasteth to his place where he arose.*

When you look at the sky and the clouds are gray
Just know in your heart they will roll away
Please keep your focus and a clear mind
Remember through out the day the sun will shine

I'm still here

Even though it seem like trials are in my way
I keep my head up cause there's a brighter day
I just stop complaining, and being doubtful all the time
When I woke this morning was clothed in my right mind
I was reminded the battle might not be for you
If you don't faint God will bring you through
For I am persuaded to let nothing on earth separate me
I'm remembering the one who hung those days on the tree
He got up with all power in the palm of his hands
With that being said now I know, and truly understand
I know how to handle tribulation when they come up
Because the Lord annointed my head, and filled my cup
So when you feel like you can't find your way
Look at the bright night always become day
Whenever the shift feels like it's stuck in the wrong gear
Say to yourself thank God on matter what "I'm stll here"

As I watch flame clouds dance in the sky
I wonder if you will come nigh
I open my mind and my ears to hear
Yes a day is coming I will be near

Exdous 33 : 21 – 22
And the Lord said, Behold, there is a place by me, and
thy shalt stand upon a rock:
And it shall come to pass, while my glory passeth by, that
I will put thee in the clift of the rock, and will
cover thee with my hand while I pass by:

Friends & Family

We all have something that ties us together
Sitting at the table or talking about the weather

As the years passes they really goes by
We are still family and friends let me tell you why

Even though things in our life they change
Our love for each other it remains the same

Even if we don't see each other every day
We are still connected in a very special way

When we call on one another, we are always there
It doesn't matter when it doesn't matter where

Family and friends are one of a kind
Own each other's hearts own each other's mind

I've leaned on you and you own me
That's how family and friends should be

So always you pray for me as I will do the same
The goodness of God we will all proclaim

As life goes on we are still family and friends
Just being there for each other has no end

So if any time we forget along the way
We'll hit the rewind button, then push play

I will

When the clouds are grey, clouds no longer blue
I will wait for the sun, until it comes through
When the rain seems it will last, and never end
I will sit back until, the next day begin
When trials come, to tear me down
I will lift myself off the sinking ground
When toubles are all around each day
I will fall on my knees, and begin to pray
When my thoughts are running wild with me
I rebuke the devil, and he will flee
When I feel like I'm in bonage again
I will pray to God, deliver the inner man
When my friends leave, I'm all alone
I will continue to gain hope, that I'll be strong
When my faith wavers and sometimes in question
I will remember God taught me a great lesson
When you have worries and troubles on your mind
I will bless te Lord. At all times

In winter when the fields are white
The moutains are a great delight
Trees are there and they stand tall
A wonderful sight of them all
Looking at them just relaxes your mind
Knowing God is with you all the time

Looking at this you would say, it's just some hay
It's the same material where Jesus did lay
As he slept the the stars shined bright
Because they knew He was the beacon light
Everyone knew and they already heard
He was the one wrap in the living word

Just remember that day breaks and night falls
The sun rises in the morning the sun set in the evening
If we wake the next day it does the same
Just be thanhful for making it one more day
Be encouragered

Photo by Lorraine Citizen

In life comes

Life is not like chocolate it's not always sweet
Purpose of the enemy to conquer and defeat
There are good days and bad ones to
It's up to you, in what you do
If you look at the ocean there my be a storm
Just remember that's where the turmoil form
I guarantee you, some rain will fall
Still watch for the rainbo as it stands tall
We have some highs, and plenty of lows
Still we learn, and continue to grow
In life comes, ups and also donws
One little smile will keep your mind sound
You might not be ready when trouble comes your wasy
Just know after midnight it's another day
Remember dark chocolate has a very different taste
You need to stay confident while you run your race
Even though you running with a very heavy load
God can deliver, our tired and weary soul

Photo by Reginald Jones

31

Growing up we all had one of these, we would swing all day and look at the trees.
We would swing and swing to reach the sky, trying to be a bird we wish we could fly.
Then one day we had to leave the swing behind, We are adults with a different mind.
Still we are able to remember the past, because good memories will always last.

When a storm comes some things stay standing others they do fall
Leaving just enough room for someone to crawl
You think to yourself "oh my where will I stay"
The storm came roaring, and it wipe the house away
My spirit is still bless I want put myself in a slope
Even though the house did fall I know there's still hope

Be encourage no matter what's going on
In Christ Jesus you will find a great home
He's always there in the time of need
A really good friend and true indeed

Many say at end a pot of gold you'll find
But trying to get there will take to much time
Remember God's promise that he made to man
He holds the covenant in the palm of His hand

46

As the sun begin to rise and you start your day
Believe anything is possible when you pray
Trials will come but they never last
Just know for yoursel4f this too shall pass

Isaiah 60: 1" Arise, shine for your light has come and the glory of the Lord has risen upon you. So do not become one who doubt. Let your light shine so that those who walk in darkness can see His glory.

What's love?

Love hung high, on cavalries cross
To and fro, Him they did toss
Love died, to give us a chance
He did it for us, in advance
Love knew one day, we would be born
They tormented Him, Him they scorn
Love didn't mumble, neither did He speak
About the ninth hour, He became weak
Love hung there till, the black of the day
After awhile the solders, Him they did lay
Love already knew, what he had to do
Was to save God's people, like me and you
Love got up, and rose to the sky
He made sure they knew, He told them why
He said it's for you, so you can live again
I got to prepare a place, so you can come in

Photo by Reginald Jones

As I stand here I don't know how I feel
Just looking beyond I begin to chill
Remembering what I was taught as a child
I start feeling better I begin to smile

Ezekiel 16: 4 " Then the glory of the Lord went up from the cherub to the threshold of the temple and the temple was filled with the cloud and the court was filled with the brightness of the glory of the Lord."

Photo by Lorraine Citizen

*"Like the appearance of a rainbow in the the clouds on a rainy day
so was the radiance of Him God gives some a double portion*

Photo by Reginald Jones

Crossing a bridge is easy to do, know who are and forever be true.
To others,to youself be a beacon light, never give up and always fight

Photo by Reginald Jones

Photo by Lorraine Citizen

Photo by Reginald Jones

Photo by Reginald Jones

I wish

I wish I could be where the rivers flow
Feel the waters when the wind starts to blow
I wish I could be where the sky stays blue
Pasting the clouds together, without the glue
I wish I could see, the stars every night
How they shine, up above oh so bright
I wish could sing, a melody of song
Feasting on a harmony, all the day long
I wish I could lie where the green grass grows
As it sparkle with color and with dew it glows
I wish I could fly, high beside the birds
I'm scared of heights don't have the nerves
I wish I could, fade the sadness away
I believe I can if I just kneel and pray
I wish I could help everyone understand
That God has given the good of the land
So if you wish and it doesn't come true
Just wait on the Lord he'll see you through

Matthew 24: 30 "And then the sign of the Son of man will appear in the sky, and then all the tribes of the earth will mourn, and they will see the Son of man coming on the cloud of the sky with power and great glory."

Along the Path

I was walking along a path one day
A man stops by and begins to say
I continue moving, going down the street
He said over and over this happen to me
I looked troubled as he begin to say
All my life storms cam my way
I found myself clinging, not knowing what to do
My friends they said what happen to you
I tried I tried I couln't say a word
My jaws was locked, my ears they still heard
Even though my lips they really couldn't speak
My mind begin to wonder, as I became weak
He said this is for you, and you should understand
God delivered me with his mighty out stretch hand
He did it for me; He can do it for you
No matter what life troubles you go through
So go ahead please and be on you way
Don't forget to thank God for another day

Rough side

There is a rough side of every mountain
Sometimes water flows like from a fountain
Even though it's rough you will be able to climb
Just grab hold to the rocks and take your time
The Lord will make your rough edges smooth
Trust and believe your moutain will move
When troubles come, and it will
Seem like a mountain it's only a mole hill
Sometimes it's not as tall as you think
Just speak the word and watch it sink
It's not going to be easy, everyday
Simply lie before God and begin to pray
Remember there's nothing new under the sun
You can bear it better if you accept the Son
Out of people lives, you they will toss
For you they will never carry a cross
So the next time in your lfe things get rough
No doubt it was Jesus, who has made you tough

Photo by Krystal Jones

Hurricane Laura came and took the tree leaves, but the tree is stilll standing it didn't fall
That's how we should be if we get brush ourself off and stand thrugh it all
Trials will come and they also will go in your season just keep the faith
Just don't give up or get weary and you'll know it was worth the wait

I feel the pain

I know that it haven't, always been good
But we can change things, and we should
Knowing how others feel, about their pain
Like having nowhere to turn, but walking on the rain
Always dark and cloudy when you look in the sky
Asking will this be over, you need to know why?
Maybe if you knew there could ever bo hope
Being alone, I'ii be able to cope
Believing in thing you can not see
Is it still possible for it to be?
You spend all day trying to clear your head
Trying to bounce back on what others said
When evening comes then we will say
Good bye morning, it's the end of the day
I still feel, what you are going through
A good night sleep you'll feel brand new
When you wake the very next day
I will ask God and he will say
Don't be discourageI heard your cry
Now I will make it better by and by

Photo by Krystal Jones

While standing I'm gazing at the sea side
Just truly grateful, on me being alive
No matter what, the vast situation
I'm looking for every indication
That I'm the product of love you see
Having my right mind knowing Jesus died for me

The sky is blue and the sun is shinning bright
Just being able to see it brings joy to my life
It also puts, a smile on my face
Just knowing I have Gods saving grace

Sometimes we fall down in life we can lay here like these tree
Or we can pull ourselves together rise up and believe
The trees don't have a choice but to lie still
Remember all things are possible it's in God's will
So the next time you stumble, trip, and you fall
Just say to yourself I know whom I can call

This is a place where we go fishing and crabing in Westlake, Louisiana feast your eyes upon this I can look at this all day. How the sun shines upon the waters as it set for the day. While you meditate just know being in that spot at that moment the sun will shine again.

Restoration is coming

Come sit with me, while I listen to the rain
Every drop that fall they are not the same
Let me encourage you, about what's going on
Please stay focus on what you always known
I know you see, what's happening today
It makes us speechless we don't know what to say
Keep looking to the hills, you'll find your help
It's He who made us, and not we ourselves
Continue holding on, to the Masters hand
Only He knows the outcome, He is the plan
I stand on His promise, and His holy word
This too shall pass, I've always heard
Keep the faith and know you're not alone
Grace and mercy will help you be strong
So keep fasting and praying it will get better
Being on your knees, worth more than any letter
Let's give God the glory, while we yet live
Restoration is coming, to us He will give

Lorner J. Jones
04/15/2020

What you see is a duck in a pond, and he's all alone
Content in just swimming it feels like home
He might be by his self are something else is there
He moving and moving like he don't care
There's no indication that he is afraid
We should be like the duck and be brave

Pray for me

When you see me coming down the street
Neither one of us, might not speak
Sometimes we feel like we are all alone
A righteous prayer will keep us strong
You really don't know how I feel
Just one ounce of prayer can truly heal
So every chance you get, please pray for me
The prayers of the righteous I really do need
When everything is going all wrong
Pray for me that I will be strong
Even when I feel I'm on the battle field
Prayer is the key my shelter and shield
Tribulations come to us every hour
Pray that I get faith, strength, and power
We all go through storms or whatever it maybe
Just always remember that Prayer is the key

Pslams 34: 1 – 8

I will bless the Lord at all times: his praise shall continually be in my mouth.
My soul shall make her boast the Lord: the humble shall hear there of, and be glad
O magnify the Lord with me, and let us exalt his name together
I sought the Lord, and he heardme, and delivered me from all my fears.
They looked unto him, and wrer enlighted: and their faces were not ashamed.
This poor man cried, and the Lord heard him, and saved him out of all his troubles
The angel of the Lord encampeth round about themthat fear him, and delivered them
O taste and see that the Lord is good: blessed is the man that trusteth in him.

Pensacola, Florida

Spanish Port

USS Alabama Battleship in Mobile

144

Psalms 121

I will lift up mine eyes unto the hills,
from whence cometh my help

My help cometh from the Lord, which
made heaven and earth.

He will not suffer they foot to be moved:
he that keepth thee will not slumber.

Behold, he that keepeth Israel shall
neither slumber nor sleep.

The Lord is thy keeper: the Lord is thy
shade upon thy right hand.

The sun shall not smite thee by day, nor the moon by night.

The Lord shall preserve thee from evil:
he shall preserve thy soul

The Lord shall preserve thy going out and thy coming
in from this time forth, and even for evermore.

Soothing is watching the sunset while you do one of your favorite things.
Enjoying the outdoors and the family times that it brings
So find what works for you for a great moment to share
Later on it will be a great memory as we sit in our rocking chair

When the sun set it is the most beautiful thing you can look at. While you are standing there all sorts of things runs through your mind. We all like to know where is the sun setting, and what city, town, state, or country did it set in. Just know God made all things well, just because we can't see it doesn't mean it didn't happen. The further you are, from the sun the longer it takes for true darkness to arrive after sundown. I want you to always remember it want be this way always

These are some of my family and friends who has served and are still serving

Kelvin Tremaine Wilkerson Sr.,
U.S. Navy (my son) deceased

Denesia Woods
U. S. Navy (my friend)

Blake Howard
U.S.Army (my friend)

Anthony Harris Sr.
U. S. Navy (my nephew)

Jamie Lynn Kelly
Williams Harris
U. S. Navy (my neice)

Leonard Frank Sallier
U.S. Army (my uncle)

Joshua Saunders
U. S. Navy (My cousin)

James Allen Owens Jr.
U. S. Army (my nephew)

James Allen Owens Sr.
U. S. Navy (my b-n-1)

James Pennix
U.S. Marines(my cousin)

Delma Bennett (drill sgt.)
U. S. Army (my cousin)

Roosevelt Trapp
U. S. Army (my friend)

Kevin Dewayne Nails
U. S. Navy (my cousin)

Calvin J. Broussard
U. S. Navy (my friend)

George Marshall Garlington
U. S. Army (my friend)

Generation of Servers from left to right
Stewart Marcantel U. S. Marines
Charles A. Marcantel U. S. Army
Justin Marcantel U. S. Army
Charles G. Marcantel U. S. Army

Derrick Dean
U.S. Army (my cousin)

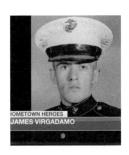

James Virgadamo was eightteen years old when he sign up for the Marines, he served from 1959 to 1971 . A few year later, he found himeself fighting against the North Vietnamese. He eventually served his tour in Vietnam and retired from the Marines in 1971. James was honored as a hometown hero in August of 2021 in Sulphur Louisiana where he resides. I think every man and woman who served and still serving should be called heros, because whether they were drafted or volunteered their lives were on the line. Some didn't make it out of that difficult situation and didn't come home to their love ones. Heros (honoring every respectable outstanding servant) . We say that we are one nation under God so let's look out and respect one another.

The Wonder Beyond

Wonder is define as: a feeling of surprise mingled with admiration, caused by something beautiful, unexpected, unfamiliar, or inexplicable.

When we write stories we write them to have an impact on someones life for the better. I write them so people can be encourage and to let them know anything is possible. Many ups will come and many downs will also ; just know the Lord will provide and He will make a way. We have all been wounded in some form or another,whether it's physical or mental. I'm a firm believer that if we hold out a change is going to come for us and everything will be alright. I truly hope you find this book of clouds and poems inspirational, because there's something about the clouds that soothes you as you stare at them. Some will say you become in awe when you look at the clouds. So I say again be encouraged and of good cheer and know that you are appreciated. I do know a long time ago when the Veterans came home they was not welcome by their Community for what reason I don't know. But it's a new day and I want all Veterans to know we appreciate your Service every Branch that served. Appreciate is define as to recognize the full worth of. It also mean grateful, and that's what I am is grateful for all of you. My favortie scripture is Psalms 34 ; I will bless Lord at all times: his praise shall contiually be in my mouth. We are one Nation under God, because he made the Heavens and the Earth and everything in it. Be a friend and help your fellow man when you can, because everybody need somebody in this world. Show them that they are needed, and to see that they are not alone. Give them their flowers while they yet live thank them while they can hear what so say. Always have some postive feed back, lend a helping hand, make a diffrence, and make it a daily task . The proceeds from this book will be donated to the Wounded Warriors Foundation we are thanking you in advance for your generosity.

Printed in the United States
by Baker & Taylor Publisher Services